ARCHIE the BEAR
THE BEACH ADVENTURE

WRITTEN BY
ROM NELSON

ILLUSTRATIONS BY
SVETLANA LESHUKOVA

Archie the Bear - The Beach Adventure
Published by The Life Graduate
www.thelifegraduate.com
Copyright © 2022 Rom Nelson
ISBN: 978-1-922664-56-3 (Paperback)
978-1-922664-55-6 (Hardback)
978-1-922664-57-0 (Ebook)

AN ORIGINAL BOOK BY

Rom Nelson

Thank you to my brilliant illustrator Svetlana for the exquisite illustrations throughout this book. You have again brought Archie the Bear to life for millions of children across the globe.

To:

My Gift to You

....

....

....

....

....

Love From ....

"Grab your sand bucket" yelled daddy from the door,
"We're off to the beach to enjoy the foreshore".

Archie was excited, the beach was always fun.
Rock pools, sandcastles and warmth from the sun.

Mommy applied the sunscreen to cover Archie's skin.
On his nose, his cheeks and under his chin.

The sun can burn when you're down by the ocean.
Archie knew the importance of applying sun lotion.

Beach towels, sand buckets and their sun-protective tent.
They all jumped in the car and off they all went.

They sang special songs about the waves and the shells,
seagulls, seaweed and those special beach smells.

They arrived at the beach and parked under a tree.

Hot car seats in summer can sting like a bee!

Archie and baby bear were so excited to explore.

There were always so many things to collect by the shore.

"Just wait right there, you must not race away".
Daddy Bear had an important rule before they play.

"Always stay close when we are down at the sea".
"This is something very important to me".

Archie grabbed the sand bucket and his little blue spade.

Sand Castles and holes were what they both made.

The seagulls stayed close, they were ready for food.

One grabbed daddy's honey sandwich; they were all very rude!

"I think we should go for a nice long walk".

"Let's get away from these seagulls and their annoying squawk".

They searched and explored the beautiful rock pools.

'Look, but don't touch'

They were rules!

Archie could see a shape that was
yellow, brown and green.
It was the most beautiful seashell
that he had ever seen!

Inside you could see a creature that
was orange and white.
It was shy and nervous and went
quickly out of sight.

"Let's head back now and have a swim before we go. It looks calm and safe and the tide is nice and low".

They splashed, they laughed, and they had so much fun.
It was the perfect beach day, enjoying the summer sun.

Archie grabbed his bucket, his beach towel and spade.
Daddy Bear folded up the umbrella that had provided the shade.

They all jumped in the car, windows down and seatbelts on.
Time to depart the beach while the sun still shone.

They all drove home as the day turned to night.
The day at the beach had been an absolute delight!

So goodbye and goodnight from Archie and baby bear.
Sometime soon they'll have a new adventure to share.

ARCHIE the BEAR

Keep an eye out for more 'Archie the Bear' books
as they are released!

Go to page 32 for current Archie the Bear Books

ABOUT THE AUTHOR

Rom Nelson is a Best Selling Author and Founder of The Life Graduate Publishing Group. He commenced his career working in some of the most well-known schools in Australia, including Head of Faculty positions in Oxford and Wimbledon, United Kingdom.

Rom authored his first book back in 2009 and has now created several books and resources, including five that have become Best Sellers in the US, UK, Canada and Australia.

The 'Archie the Bear' Series has been created for toddlers in a fun and enjoyable hand-drawn picture storybook format, helping them to prepare for new experiences.

Using fun and creative rhyming language, Archie the Bear will help parents by taking their children through the experience so they are prepared and relaxed.

Romney Nelson

ARCHIE the BEAR

ADVENTURES

JOIN ARCHIE AS HE SHOWS TODDLERS HOW TO USE THE POTTY!

POTTY TRAINING

amazon

Made in United States
Orlando, FL
23 May 2023